It's Ok To Be Single

A Book of Declarations:
VOLUME 1 – ALL ABOUT ME!

M.A. Jackson

Copyright © 2021 by **M.A. Jackson**

All rights reserved. No part of this publication may be reproduced by any means, graphics, electronic, or mechanical, including photocopying, recording, taping, or by any information storage retrieval system without the written permission of the publisher except in the case of brief quotations embodied in critical articles and reviews.

M.A. Jackson/Rejoice Essential Publishing
PO BOX 512
Effingham, SC 29541

www.republishing.org

Unless otherwise indicated, scripture is taken from the King James Version.

Scripture quotations marked (NIV) are taken from the Holy Bible, New International Version®, NIV®. Copyright © 1973, 1978, 1984, 2011 by Biblica, Inc.™ Used by permission of Zondervan. All rights reserved worldwide. www.zondervan.com The "NIV" and "New International Version" are trademarks registered in the United States Patent and Trademark Office by Biblica, Inc.™

Scripture taken from the New King James Version®. Copyright © 1982 by Thomas Nelson. Used by permission. All rights reserved.

The Holy Bible, Berean Study Bible, BSB Copyright ©2016, 2018 by Bible Hub Used by Permission. All Rights Reserved Worldwide.

Scripture quotations marked (ESV) are taken from The Holy Bible,

English Standard Version® (ESV®) Copyright © 2001 by Crossway, a publishing ministry of Good News Publishers. All rights reserved.

"Scripture quotations taken from the (NASB®) New American Standard Bible®, Copyright © 1960, 1971, 1977, 1995, 2020 by The Lockman Foundation. Used by permission. All rights reserved. www.lockman.org"

Scripture quotations marked (NLT) are taken from the Holy Bible, New Living Translation, copyright ©1996, 2004, 2015 by Tyndale House Foundation. Used by permission of Tyndale House Publishers, Carol Stream, Illinois 60188. All rights reserved.

Scripture quotations marked (GNT) are from the Good News Translation in Today's English Version- Second Edition Copyright © 1992 by American Bible Society. Used by Permission.

It's Ok To Be Single/ M. A. Jackson

ISBN-13: 978-1-952312-74-8

Library of Congress Control Number: 2021910159

Dedication

This book is dedicated to God first because He kept me in my singleness. Even when I struggled, He was right there, holding my hand. I also want to dedicate this book to all the people who encouraged me to write this book.

CONTENTS

ACKNOWLEDGMENTS..ix

INTRODUCTION...1

CHAPTER ONE: Self-Care..............................3

CHAPTER TWO: Dealing with
                       Loneliness.........................12

CHAPTER THREE: Dealing with
                       Forgiveness.......................28

CHAPTER FOUR: Let it Go!...........................42

CHAPTER FIVE: Dealing with
                       Rejection..........................55

CHAPTER SIX: Dealing with
                       Coveting............................67

CHAPTER SEVEN: Dealing with Word
                       Curses...............................80

CHAPTER 8:	Dealing with Thoughts	94
CHAPTER 9:	Fasting and Praying	101
CHAPTER 10:.	Getting to Know You	108
CHAPTER 11:.	Single's Opportunities	120
CHAPTER 12:.	The I am Code	127
CHAPTER 13:	Wait	135
ABOUT THE AUTHOR		137

Acknowledgments

I want to thank my family for supporting me to walk in my gifts. I also want to thank my mentor, Prophetess Kimberly Moses, for encouraging me to write this book. She has pulled out of me many skills through love, prayer, and coaching. I thank God for allowing us to cross paths.

Introduction

SPEAK OVER YOURSELF.

Philippians 2:9-11 (NKJV) says, "Therefore God exalted him to the highest place and gave him the name that is above every name, that at the name of Jesus every knee should bow, in heaven and on earth and under the earth, and every tongue acknowledge that Jesus Christ is LORD, to the glory of God the Father."

The name of Jesus Christ is over every situation that is in your life. So, when you end a prayer (decree, declaration, rebuke, bind, will, claim, reclaim, cancellation, command, denounce, renounce, condemn, cast out, etc.) with the name of Jesus Christ attached to it, EVERY knee has to bow and pay attention to your concerns. Once that power source is on, things WILL have to change.

CHAPTER ONE

Self-Care

Sometimes you have to look in the mirror and ask yourself, "Am I taking care of myself?" If you answered NO, then self-care is what you lack in your life. Self-care is the practice of taking an active role in protecting your well-being and happiness. These are two powerful words that can change your entire life for the better.

Sometimes you can forget about yourself due to life's demands and the demands of others. You ignore warning signs, red flags, the cries of the spirit, body, soul, and we keep going to ensure everything around us continues to flow. Self-care is not a selfish act; it's more like an investment in your health and well-being.

Self-care has many different categories. These include personal hygiene, healthy eating habits, getting a good night's sleep, exercising, making time for social events, paying attention to your thoughts and feelings, and many other things that have meaning to you. It would be best if you make sure you haven't forgotten about yourself.

You can't help someone else if you're not taking care of yourself!

I decree that I will take time out to self-care daily in the name of Jesus Christ.

I cancel self-neglect in the name of Jesus Christ.

I desire to love myself in the name of Jesus Christ.

I will give You thanks in the great congregation; I will praise You among a mighty throne. — Psalm 35:18

Thank you, Jesus Christ, for loving me.

Thank you, Father, for caring for me first in the name of Jesus Christ.

Thank you, Father, for giving me the ability to take care of myself in the name of Jesus Christ.

Love the Lord your God with all your heart and with all your soul and with all your mind and with all your strength. The second is this: 'Love your neighbor as yourself.' There is no commandment greater than these. —Mark 12:30-31 (NIV).

Thank you, Father, for giving me the ability to love and take care of myself so that I can take care of others.

So in everything, do to others what you would have them do to you, for this sums up the Law and the Prophets. — Matthew 7:12 (NIV).

I decree that I will treat everyone righteously in the name of Jesus Christ.

A new command I give you: Love one another. As I have loved you, so you must love one another. By this everyone will know that you are my disciples if you love one another." — John 13:34-35 (NIV).

I claim that love flows through me in the name of Jesus Christ.

I cancel self-belittling in the name of Jesus Christ.

I will have self-belief in the name of Jesus Christ.

I decree that the way I provide care for others is how I will provide for myself in the power of the mighty name of Jesus Christ.

This Book of the Law shall not depart from your mouth, but you shall meditate on it day and night, so that you may be careful to do according to all that is written in it. For then, you will make your way prosperous, and then you will have success. — Joshua 1:8 (NIV).

I will meditate on the Word of God daily in the name of Jesus Christ.

I will take measures to get things off my chest safely in the name of Jesus Christ.

I will laugh more often in the name of Jesus Christ.

I will exercise so that my body can be fit to do the works of the Lord.

I desire to eat healthy with lots of greens daily.

I decree that I will take a break when I need it.

I decree that I will learn to say, "No."

I am just as important as the next person; therefore, I will treat myself to something special.

I will pay attention to my thoughts and feelings.

I claim that I will keep myself full of giving fullness to those I am caring for in the name of Jesus Christ.

I will honor myself with self-care in the name of Jesus Christ.

I denounce depleting and overwhelming myself in the name of Jesus Christ.

I will stop and ask God what I need to do before I agree to more work.

I am exquisite and extraordinary in the name of Jesus Christ.

I choose to love myself in the name of Jesus Christ.

I choose to honor myself in the name of Jesus Christ.

I choose to listen to wisdom.

I choose to care for myself in the name of Jesus Christ.

I claim that I will acknowledge the red flags and take heed in the name of Jesus Christ.

I am a blessing in the name of Jesus Christ.

I am a blessing in the name of Jesus Christ.

I am assertive with the presence of God.

I denounce overthinking in the name of Jesus Christ

I decree that I will relax more.

I claim a good night's sleep in the name of Jesus Christ.

I decree I will visit my loved ones more often.

I denounce overwhelming myself with other problems.

I know that You are the mighty God that can fix all situations.

I decree that I will not cut corners when it comes to me in the name of Jesus Christ.

I denounce physical and emotional exhaustion due to long term care.

I will keep myself full of myself, so I have enough overfull to give to others in the name of Jesus Christ.

I will keep my gifts sharp to offer them to others in the name of Jesus Christ.

I claim I will do things that will keep me healthy in the name of Jesus Christ.

I will seek relief for myself when I am under pressure and stress in the name of Jesus Christ.

I decree that I will have self-respect for myself in the name of Jesus Christ.

I decree that others will have respect for me in the name of Jesus Christ.

I decree that I will do things that make me feel relaxed, joyful, and peaceful.

I decree that I will take on an attitude that says, "My needs deserve attention too."

I will invest in myself while caring for others.

I will manage stress safely in the name of Jesus Christ.

Today is the first day of many days I will take just for me!   Amen.

Father, in the name of Jesus Christ, I bless and praise thee Oh God. I decree and declare that I will take care of me by…

_____

_____

_____

_____

_____

_____

_____

_____

_____

_____

_____

_____

_____

_____

_____

_____

_____

_____

CHAPTER TWO

Dealing with Loneliness

Loneliness is an emotional state of mind when feeling disconnected. It is something that every person perceives from time to time, and it can be recognized early in some cases. It could also be deeply rooted and undetected, which can lead to depression and affect your health. When some people feel alone, they want to be surrounded with friends they can trust, but that is not the antidote.

Loneliness comes from a lack of security and wanting to belong. It is growing in our society as people are becoming more isolated with new technology. Even though we have access to people at the push of a button, people still deal with some loneliness.

Gladly, you can fight against the spirit of loneliness with the Word of God and surrounding yourself with loving friends that can help you get through it. So when you feel the spirit of loneliness arising, don't let it linger; immediately bind it up with the Word of God.

I reject the spirit of loneliness and cast it in the abyss in the name of Jesus Christ.

I decree that I have overcome loneliness in the name of Jesus Christ.

O give thanks unto the LORD; call upon his name: make known his deeds among the people. — Psalms 105:1

Thank you, Father, for removing the sadness out of my life.

Thank you, Father, for giving me real friends in the name of Jesus Christ.

Thank you, Father, for removing the spirit of loneliness around me.

I will declare that God has delivered me from the spirit of loneliness.

Hear me when I call, O God of my righteousness: thou hast enlarged me when I was in distress; have mercy upon me and hear my prayer. — Psalms 4:1

I desire for loneliness to go in the name of Jesus Christ.

Trust in the Lord with all thine heart, and lean not unto thine own understanding. In all thy ways acknowledge Him, and he shall direct thy paths. — Proverbs 3:5-6

I bind up any evil thoughts in my mind in the name of Jesus Christ.

For the weapons of our warfare are not carnal, but mighty through God to the pulling down of strongholds; — 2 Corinthians 10:4

I cancel loneliness in the name of Jesus Christ.

I cancel out anything or anyone that possesses loneliness in the name of Jesus Christ.

I speak peace in my life in the name of Jesus Christ.

Be strong and courageous. Do not be afraid or terrified because of them, for the LORD your God goes with you; he will never leave you nor forsake you." — Deuteronomy 31:6 (BSB)

I will not focus on the negative thoughts in the name of Jesus Christ.

I will seek Godly advice on getting out of loneliness.

I claim the strength of the Father in my life.

I will not be afraid in the name of Jesus Christ.

Though my Father and mother forsake me, the LORD will receive me.— Psalm 27:10 (NIV)

I know that I am not alone because Jesus Christ is with me.

Many may leave my side, but my Father will always be around me.

For the sake of his great name, the LORD will not reject his people, because the LORD was pleased to make you his own. — 1 Samuel 12:22 (NIV)

I decree that I will not let rejection enter my life in the name of Jesus Christ.

I desire favor in my life in the name of Jesus Christ.

I will move on from those who reject me in the name of Jesus Christ.

I will shake the dust off my feet to those who do not accept me for me in the name of Jesus Christ.

I decree that I will make eye contact with people in the name of Jesus Christ.

I will not get sick over loneliness in the name of Jesus Christ.

Turn to me and be gracious to me, for I am lonely and afflicted.— Psalm 25:16 (NIV)

I decree that God will hear my heart's cry and comfort me in the name of Jesus Christ.

I denounce the lack of companionship in the name of Jesus Christ.

I denounce isolation from other people.

I decree that I will surround myself with like-minded people in the name of Jesus.

I claim that I will not feel left out in the name of Jesus Christ.

I claim that the people that surround me will know who I am in the name of Jesus Christ.

I claim that other people understand me in the name of Jesus Christ.

I claim that my surroundings support me.

I thank the Father for blessing me with people I can talk to within the name of Jesus Christ.

I claim that the Father will send people I can turn to in Jesus Christ name.

I claim a refreshing in the name of Jesus Christ.

I know that I am not alone because I have the Holy Ghost by my side.

Fear not, for I am with you; be not dismayed, for I am your God; I will strengthen you, I will help you, I will uphold you with my righteous right hand. — Isaiah 41:10 (NKJV)

Be strong and courageous. Do not fear or be in dread of them, for it is the Lord your God who goes with you. He will not leave you or forsake you." — Deuteronomy 31:6 (ESV)

I know that God is with me, and the spirit of loneliness is defeated.

No weapon that is formed against thee shall prosper, and every tongue that shall rise against thee in judgment thou shalt condemn. This is the heritage of the servants of the Lord, and their righteousness is of me, saith the Lord. — Isaiah 54:17

I will be strong in the Lord, and loneliness will not come near my dwelling.

Come to Me, all you who labor and are heavy laden, and I will give you rest. — Matthew 11:28 (NKJV)

I will give the Lord all my burdens in the name of Jesus Christ.

I will take on the easy yoke of Jesus Christ.

I declare that I will have rest in the name of Jesus Christ.

Then the Lord God said, "It is not good that the man should be alone; I will make him a helper fit for him." — Genesis 2:18 (ESV)

In the name of Jesus Christ, Father, I thank you for not leaving me alone.

Father, I thank you for surrounding me with the people who are fit for me this season.

Casting all your anxieties on Him, because he cares for you. — 1 Peter 5:7 (NIV)

"I will not leave you as orphans; I will come to you. — John 14:18 (NIV)

Do not be anxious about anything, but in everything by prayer and supplication with thanksgiving, let your requests be made known to God. And the peace of God, which surpasses all understanding, will guard your hearts and your minds in Christ Jesus. — Philippians 4:6-7 (ESV)

I will not suffer from the spirit of loneliness in the name of Jesus Christ.

"Fear not, for I have redeemed you; I have called you by your name; you are Mine. When you pass through the waters, I will be with you; And through the rivers, they shall not overflow you. When you walk through the fire, you shall not be burned, nor shall the flame scorch you." — Isaiah 43:1-2 (NKJV)

I will not take on other people's problems in the name of Jesus Christ.

The Lord God rebuke depression in the name of Jesus Christ.

The LORD is my strength and my shield; my heart trusts in Him, and he helps me. My heart leaps for joy, and with my song, I praise Him. — Psalm 28:7 (NIV)

Stand fast therefore in the liberty wherewith Christ hath made us free, and be not entangled again with the yoke of bondage. — Galatians 5:1

I will accept God's will for my life.

I will stop blaming others for my faults in the name of Jesus Christ.

I will not worry about tomorrow. I will trust in the Lord.

I will not doubt the Word of God.

I will read the Word of God to strengthen my soul in the name of Jesus Christ.

I will have confidence in God and be secure in His provision for my life.

I will change my thoughts and think on things above in the name of Jesus Christ.

I will embrace a new attitude in Jesus Christ name.

I will call on wisdom in the name of Jesus Christ.

I will do something that will keep my mind in a positive state.

Not giving up meeting together, as some are in the habit of doing, but encouraging one another-and all the more as you see the day approaching. If we deliberately keep on sinning after we have received the knowledge of the truth, no sacrifice for sins is left. — Hebrews 10:25-26 (NIV)

I decree that I will not miss an opportunity to meet new people in the name of Jesus Christ.

I decree that this is my time to shine with friends in the name of Jesus Christ.

I decree that I will not use excuses to isolate myself in the name of Jesus Christ.

I decree that I will be friendly in the name of Jesus Christ.

I claim that I will be more responsive to other people in the name of Jesus Christ.

I desire to be in good company and be a good company in the name of Jesus Christ.

I decree I will encourage myself as well as others in the name of Jesus Christ.

Thank you, Lord, for not abandoning me in the good and the bad times of life.

Thank you, Father, for keeping me in a social setting.

And it shall come to pass in that day, that his burden shall be taken away from off thy shoulder, and his yoke from off thy neck, and the yoke shall be destroyed because of the anointing.— Isaiah 10:27

I declare that the anointing of God is upon me.

I declare that I am victorious.

I declare I will speak positive words of faith over my life.

I decree I will thrive.

I decree I have everything I need in the name of Jesus Christ.

I decree that my faith will strengthen through Jesus Christ.

I decree and declare that all things are working for my good.

I claim many blessings over my life in the name of Jesus Christ.

I declare a breakthrough is coming to my life.

I desire joyfulness in my life in the name of Jesus Christ.

I desire peacefulness in the name of Jesus Christ.

I denounce the thought of being lonely in the name of Jesus Christ.

Father, clean my heart and renew my mind in the name of Jesus Christ.

In the name of Jesus Christ, Father, prepare me for future events in my life.

Loneliness has no power over my mind, body, nor my soul.

I decree when the spirit of loneliness comes my way, the Spirit of the Lord will eliminate it.

The Lord, thy God, rebuke the spirit of loneliness in the name of Jesus Christ.

I decree my life is now made brand new. Amen.

Father, in the name of Jesus Christ, I thank You and praise You, my God. I decree and declare that I will not let loneness get the best of me. I will…

_____
_____
_____
_____
_____
_____
_____
_____
_____
_____
_____
_____
_____
_____
_____
_____
_____
_____

CHAPTER THREE

Dealing with Forgiveness

Forgiveness, what does that mean to you? Forgiveness is a process with no set time rules or limits. Forgiveness doesn't mean forgetting or excusing the offense; it is the intentional process that changes feelings, attitudes and overcoming negative emotions such as resentment and vengeance. We often want to get the offender back, but it would be best to leave it in the hands of God. "Repay no one evil for evil. Have regard for good things in the sight of all men. If it is possible, as much as depends on you, live peaceably with all men. Beloved, do not avenge yourselves, but rather give place to wrath; for it is written, "Vengeance is Mine, I will repay," says the Lord (Romans 12:19)."

Matthew 5:43-45 states, "You have heard that it was said, 'Love your neighbor and hate your enemy. But I tell you, love your enemies and pray for those who persecute you, that you may be children of your Father in heaven." When you pray blessings over your enemies, God will bless them to receive the revelation on the offense they committed towards you. They will come face to face with the truth and deal with it. God is asking you to pray blessings for your sake.

After you have prayed blessings over your enemies, it doesn't mean that the pain vanishes instantly. It means that you have done your part. Now you can remind God that you overcame evil with good, and He is free to have His way concerning the matter.

Forgiving yourself is also needed in your life. Everyone makes mistakes, but God's love for us covers our errors. There is, therefore, now no condemnation for those who are in Christ Jesus (Romans 8:1 ESV).

I reject the spirit of unforgiveness and cast it into the abyss, unable to return in the name of Jesus Christ.

For if you forgive other people when they sin against you, your heavenly Father will also forgive you. 15 But if you do not forgive others their sins, your Father will not forgive your sins. — Matthew 6:14-15 (NIV)

Thank you, Father, for forgiving me of all my sin.

Thank you for your undeserved mercy.

Thank you, Father, for teaching me how to deal with forgiveness.

Thank you, Jesus Christ, for being the most excellent example to show us how to forgive.

Cast all your anxieties on Him, because He cares for you. — 1 Peter 5:7 (ESV)

In the name of Jesus Christ, Father, please teach me the power of forgiveness.

Thank you, Father, for letting me give all my cares to You.

Father, I am ready to rip down the walls in my heart and walk in Your promise.

Father, please forgive me for hurting other people.

Thank you, Holy Ghost, for guiding me through my troubles.

I choose to forgive in the name of Jesus Christ.

I choose to forgive those who hurt me in Jesus Christ name.

I choose to forgive myself in the name of Jesus Christ.

I will forgive, so I will not have unexpected aftermath in the name of Jesus Christ.

Father, in the name of Jesus Christ, I choose Your way.

I will forgive those who have offended me in the name of Jesus Christ.

I decree that I will pray blessings over my enemies in the name of Jesus Christ.

I decree that I will have the heart to forgive in the name of Jesus Christ.

Therefore, if anyone is in Christ, he is a new creation. The old has passed away; behold, the new has come. — 2 Corinthians 5:17 (ESV)

He does not deal with us according to our sins, nor repay us according to our iniquities. For as high as the heavens are above the earth, so great is his steadfast love toward those who fear him. — Psalm 103:10-11 (ESV)

There is, therefore, now no condemnation for those who are in Christ Jesus. — Romans 8:1 (ESV)

I declare that I will not look down on myself for making a mistake in Jesus' name.

But this one thing I do, forgetting those things which are behind, and reaching forth unto those things which are before. — Philippians 3:13

We all fall short of the Glory of God. — Romans 3:23

I decree that I will look towards my future in the name of Jesus Christ.

I acknowledged my [mistakes] to You… and You forgave [them]. — Psalm 32:5

I decree that I will pray for those who offended me in the name of Jesus Christ.

I decree that the Holy Ghost will help me make the right decisions in my life.

I declare that all my tears of sorrow are now joy in the name of Jesus Christ.

I decree that every limitation be removed now in the name of Jesus Christ.

I forgive them in the name of Jesus Christ.

I am restored now from all hurt in the name of Jesus Christ.

I rebuke all who oppose my restoration in the name of Jesus Christ.

I claim that God will give me blessings for my troubles.

I will not lock myself in the past where there is unforgiveness in the name of Jesus Christ.

I will not be petty and impulsive in the name of Jesus Christ.

I will not bottle up anger in the name of Jesus Christ.

I prophesy that I will have a peaceful environment.

I prophesy that this will be a blessed year in the name of Jesus Christ.

I prophesy that I will have perfect peace in the name of Jesus Christ.

I prophesy that my love for others will increase in the name of Jesus Christ.

I prophesy that I will achieve every goal I put forth in the name of Jesus Christ.

I claim that I will acquire everything back the enemy stole.

I reject a life of not forgiving others in the name of Jesus Christ.

I bind up relationships that will vex my soul in the name of Jesus Christ.

I decree that I will have thicker skin in the name of Jesus Christ.

I decree that I will not let negative things linger in my mind in the name of Jesus Christ.

I ask for joy over my life in the name of Jesus Christ.

I ask for peace over my life in the name of Jesus Christ.

I ask for love upon my life in the name of Jesus Christ.

Father, please help me to let go of all the wrong decisions in my life.

I claim the courage to let go of strongholds in my life.

So watch yourselves. "If your brother or sister sins against you, rebuke them; and if they repent, forgive them. 4 Even if they sin against you seven times in a day and seven times come back to you saying 'I repent,' you must forgive them." — Luke 17:3-4 (NIV)

Father, in the name of Jesus Christ, I repent of my sins.

I claim that I will forgive a person seventy times seven in the name of Jesus Christ.

I will not gossip about them or the situation in the name of Jesus Christ.

I claim that I will not keep a record of the hurt in my life in the name of Jesus Christ.

Get rid of all bitterness, rage, and anger, brawling and slander, along with every form of malice. 32 Be kind and compassionate to one another, forgiving each other, just as in Christ God forgave you. — Ephesians 4:31-32 (ESV)

I bind up recalling the past offenses in the name of Jesus Christ.

I desire brighter days ahead of me.

If we confess our sins, he is faithful and just and will forgive us our sins and purify us from all unrighteousness.— John 1:9 (NIV)

I forgive myself.

I will not hate myself in the name of Jesus Christ.

I will not over or under-eat in the name of Jesus Christ.

I rebuke, replaying the offense over and over in my head.

I will forgive and keep moving in the name of Jesus Christ.

I rebuke brokenness inside of me in the name of Jesus Christ.

I will practice forgiveness in my everyday life.

I will make forgiveness a habit in my life in the mighty name of Jesus Christ.

I will seek help if I need it.

I rebuke the hurt and emotions that are attached to unforgiveness in the name of Jesus Christ.

I will not let unforgiveness destroy my life in the name of Jesus Christ.

I will let go of unforgiveness.

I release all the hurt in the name of Jesus Christ.

Now that I have forgiven, I will have joy back in my life.

In the name of Jesus Christ, Father, please forgive me for having unforgiving manners.

Thank you for delivering me from the Kingdom of darkness.

Bear with each other and forgive one another if any of you has a grievance against someone. Forgive as the Lord forgave you. — Colossians 3:13 (NIV)

I claim a heart to forgive in the name of Jesus Christ.

I release feelings of resentment or vengeance toward my offenses in the name of Jesus Christ.

Therefore, if anyone is in Christ, the new creation has come: The old has gone, the new is here! — 2 Corinthians 5:17 (NIV)

Because I deserve peace, I will forgive in the name of Jesus Christ.

And we know that in all things, God works for the good of those who love him, who have been called according to his purpose. — Romans 8:28 (NIV)

Father, in the name of Jesus Christ, I bless and praise thee Oh God. I decree and declare that I will forgive them from…

CHAPTER FOUR

Let it Go

So, the relationship that went wrong let it go. The relationship that's not happening right now, let it go. The people who did you wrong, let it go. The money they stole from you, let that go. The scars they left you with, mend them up and let them go.

Three simple words carry a great deal of weight and express the notion to stop thinking or being upset over something or somebody. When you hold on to negativity, you will be the one that is suffering behind it. It's time to create a better you! Focus on what you can do today to stay committed to your future.

You are strong enough to let go and live your life fully regardless of what happened or what it could have been. The best thing to do is the move on and let God have His way.

I reject the spirit of not letting go and cast it into the abyss in the name of Jesus Christ.

In the name of Jesus Christ, Father, I thank you for allowing me to let go of past relationships.

≈

I will accept that the relationship is over in the name of Jesus Christ.

I rebuke a reconnection to unfruitful relationships in the name of Jesus Christ.

If I can't get over them, Father let them get over me in the name of Jesus Christ.

I claim a better relationship in the future in the name of Jesus Christ.

I will not have the title of "just friends." I decree that it is over in all areas in the name of Jesus Christ.

I denounce Exodus 14:5-6, which states, "When the king of Egypt was told that the people had fled, Pharaoh and his officials changed their minds about them and said, "What have we done? We have let the Israelites go and have lost their services!" So he had his chariot made ready and took his army with him."

I will not change my mind; I will let go in the name of Jesus Christ.

I denounce asking my friends to help me get back into old relationships.

I denounce giving my services to my old relationships in the name of Jesus Christ.

Thank you, Lord, for setting me free in the name of Jesus Christ.

Thank you for moving me forward in the name of Jesus Christ.

I have let go to receive something new in the name of Jesus Christ.

Dearly beloved, avenge not yourselves, but rather give place unto wrath: for it is written, vengeance is mine; I will repay, saith the Lord. — Romans 12:19

I will let go of all thoughts of evil and revenge in the name of Jesus Christ.

I will not seek revenge in the name of Jesus Christ.

I will not stalk my ex's social media sites in the name of Jesus Christ.

I will reflect on the things I can change about myself in the name of Jesus Christ.

I will remove special items that remind me of past relationships around me in the name of Jesus Christ.

I let go of all regrets in the name of Jesus Christ.

I forgive myself for getting involved with a person that was not sent by the Father.

Father, I thank You for releasing me from soul ties.

The Lord is not slow to fulfill his promise as some count slowness, but is patient toward you, not wishing that any should perish, but that all should reach repentance. — 2 Peter 3:9 (ESV)

I will not rush into another relationship in the name of Jesus Christ.

I decree that the Lord will lead me to my spouse.

I claim that I will take care of myself during the breakup process in the name of Jesus Christ.

In the name of Jesus Christ, Father, bless me to let go and move on.

In Luke 10:19, "Christ declared, Behold, I give unto you power to tread on serpents and scorpions and over all the enemy's power: and nothing shall by any means hurt you."

So shall they fear the name of the Lord from the west, and his glory from the rising of the sun? When the enemy shall come in like a flood, the Spirit of the

Lord shall lift up a standard against him.— Isaiah 59:19

I will release the memories of past experiences in the name of Jesus Christ.

I will release the past to move on in the future in the name of Jesus Christ.

I will let go of past hurts in the name of Jesus Christ.

I will let go of those who don't see my worth in the name of Jesus Christ.

I will let go of those who angered me in the name of Jesus Christ.

I let go of my bad attitude in the name of Jesus Christ.

I will let the past stay in the past in the name of Jesus Christ.

They went out from us, but they did not really belong to us. For if they had belonged to us, they would have remained with us; but their going showed that none of them belonged to us. — 1 John 2:19 (NIV)

I will keep going in Jesus Christ name.

I will let go of controlling others' actions in the name of Jesus Christ.

I will not expect someone to support me in Jesus Christ name.

I expect the things that I cannot change.

I will get better after any bad situation in the name of Jesus Christ.

I will no longer be stuck in this place any longer.

I denounce being mad and sad in the name of Jesus Christ.

People gave up on me, but God is still using me.

Then He who sat on the throne said, "Behold, I make all things new." And He said to me, "Write, for these words are true and faithful." — Revelation 21:5 (NKJV)

Not that I have already obtained all this, or have already arrived at my goal, but I press on to take hold of that for which Christ Jesus took hold of me. Brothers and sisters, I do not consider myself yet to have taken hold of it. But one thing I do: Forgetting what is behind and straining toward what is ahead, I press on toward the goal to win the prize for which God has called me heavenward in Christ Jesus. Philippians — 3:12-14 (NIV)

Now unto him, that is able to do exceeding abundantly above all that we ask or think, according to the power that worketh in us, Unto him be glory in the church by Christ Jesus throughout all ages, world without end. Amen. — Ephesians 3:20-21

Everything is coming is better than what I am leaving.

I will release regrets in the name of Jesus Christ.

I will focus on the new season in Jesus Christ name.

I love myself.

My brethren, count it all joy when ye fall into divers temptations; — James 1:2

I will shift my focus on things I have gained in the name of Jesus Christ.

What happened in my past has prepared me for now.

I will cut off all contact with persons that keep my mind in bondage in the name of Jesus Christ.

I will have growth, peace, and happiness in the name of Jesus Christ.

I will know love again.

I will trust love again.

I will have friends that will help me get to a breakthrough in the name of Jesus Christ.

Father, please allow me to see the way you see me.

I will open myself up to the path God has prepared for me.

This year will set up the best years for the rest of my life.

I will flourish in my calling.

I will close the doors and move on.

I will let myself mourn in the name of Jesus Christ.

I am healed in Jesus Christ name.

I will bless and move on.

I will let all hope go in the name of Jesus Christ.

I will expect what happened and move on towards the future.

I will read books on how to let go.

I will seek professional help if I need it.

I will not focus on social media.

I will let go so I can have peace in the name of Jesus Christ.

I will be open to new possibilities.

I will replace fearful thoughts with hopeful thoughts.

I will love again.

I am no longer lonely.

I am powerful.

All pain passes with time.

And may the Lord cause you to increase and overflow with love for one another and for everyone, just as we do for you. — 1 Thessalonians 3:12 (NASB)

I will control the way I respond to hurt and pain.

I will speak positive affirmations over myself every day.

I will renew my mind daily.

I will pray over myself daily.

I will press through.

I will fast and pray for the things that keep me in bondage.

I will spend more time with God.

I will release people that God has instructed me to let go of in the name of Jesus Christ.

I will learn from all past experiences.

I will accept that the relationship is over, and I am free to move on in Jesus Christ name.

I forgive myself and others that have hurt me.

I accept my part in the broken relationship.

I press toward the mark for the prize of the high calling of God in Christ Jesus. — Philippians 3:14

Father in the name of Jesus Christ, I bless and praise thee Oh God. I decree and declare that I will let go of...

_____

_____

CHAPTER FIVE

Dealing with Rejection

Refusal, turning down, declining, dismissal, spurning, rebuff, knock-back, non-acceptance, denial, veto, exclusion, abandonment, spurning, casting off, disowning, thumbs down, renunciation, repudiation, eschew, these are words that stem from rejection. Rejection is something many people experience, and it hurts. It can make you give up and feel like a failure or not valuable. But there is good news; you can overcome rejection through God's Word, which brings confidence and patience.

God gave you a purpose for His ultimate plan, so put forth your best self and leave the rest in the hands of the Father.

I reject the spirit of rejection and cast it into the abyss not to return in the name of Jesus Christ.

I command every spirit of rejection to come out of me right now in the name of Jesus Christ.

I command the spirit for self-rejection to leave me alone and do not return in the name of Jesus Christ.

I receive acceptance from the Father.

I forgive everyone that offended me in the name of Jesus Christ.

I ask you to please forgive my enemies and bless them by the power of Jesus Christ.

I decree a swift turnaround in the name of Jesus Christ.

I decree a great future ahead of me in the name of Jesus Christ.

And we know that all things work together for good to them that love God, to them who are the called according to [his] purpose. — Romans 8:28

I claim that the rejection will work for my good in the name of Jesus Christ.

I know that God will work things together for His glory and my benefit in the name of Jesus Christ.

I know that I am called for His purpose in the name of Jesus Christ.

I know that my God will supply every need of mine according to His riches in glory in Christ Jesus.

I break the power of disease in the name of Jesus Christ.

He came unto his own, and his own received him not. — John 1:11

What shall we then say to these things? If God be for us, who can be against us? — Romans 8:31

This is the confidence we have in approaching God: that if we ask anything according to his will, he hears us. — 1 John 5:14

I ask that the spirit of rejection scatter in the name of Jesus Christ.

I command that every spirit that torments me be removed by the power of Jesus Christ.

I break the power of any demonic spirits that are causing problems in my life and command them to leave by the power of Jesus Christ.

I claim that Christ Jesus will lift my spirit and make me whole again.

I claim the peace of God in my life, which surpasses all understanding.

Blessed are ye, when men shall hate you, and when they shall separate you [from their company], and shall reproach [you], and cast out your name as evil, for the Son of man's sake. — Luke 6:22

I am still blessed even amid rejection in the name of Jesus Christ.

I am not forgotten; God has a plan for my breakthrough.

Every disappointment has been just a set up for my good in Jesus Christ name.

I decree that God will vindicate me.

I claim my Godly identity in the name of Jesus Christ.

Surely, he hath borne our griefs, and carried our sorrows: yet we did esteem him stricken, smitten of God, and afflicted. — Isaiah 53:4

And whosoever shall not receive you, nor hear your words, when ye depart out of that house or city, shake off the dust of your feet. — Matthew 10:14

I decree I will not look back on the people who did not receive me in the name of Jesus Christ.

I claim that I will not be pushed aside by the power of Jesus Christ.

When my Father and my mother forsake me, then the LORD will take me up. — Psalms 27:10

For I know the thoughts that I think toward you, saith the LORD, thoughts of peace, and not of evil, to give you an expected end. — Jeremiah 29:11

Can a woman forget her sucking child, that she should not have compassion on the son of her womb? Yea, they may forget, yet will I not forget thee.— Isaiah 49:15

Thank you, Father, for not forgetting me.
I will acknowledge my emotions in the name of Jesus Christ.

I declare that I will not take rejection personally in the name of Jesus Christ.

I claim the rejection saved me from hard aches and pain in the name of Jesus Christ.

I claim I will treat myself with compassion in Jesus Christ name.

I declare I will take up a hobby.

I denounce word curses from my parents that brought on rejection in the name of Jesus Christ.

I claim that people will hear what I have to say in the name of Jesus Christ.

I am loved in the name of Jesus Christ.

I declare when someone consistently tells me, "No," I know that God is working for my good.

I rebuke the spirit of abandonment in the name of Jesus Christ.

I rebuke sadness in the name of Jesus Christ.

I bind social rejection in the name of Jesus Christ.

I will overcome every negative emotion that came from rejection in the name of Jesus Christ.

I will control my reaction when I get rejected.

I will increase my self-esteem in the name of Jesus Christ.

I will focus on what I have accomplished in my life in the name of Jesus Christ.

I will rise above the negativity in the name of Jesus Christ.

I will reach out to meet positive and like-minded people.

I will not be afraid of rejections in the name of Jesus Christ.

I will face the pain of the rejections that are before me.

I am healed from rejection in the name of Jesus Christ.

I know that I am unique in my Father's eyes.

I know all the things you do, and I have opened a door for you that no one can close. You have little strength, yet you obeyed my word and did not deny me. — Revelation 3:8 (NLT)

In the name of Jesus Christ, Father, thank you for providing an open door to overcome rejection.

I choose to release the rejection and move on in the name of Jesus Christ.

Rejection is a useful redirection in my life. My God has something greater for my future.

I decree the next opportunity will blow my mind, and I apply the blood of Jesus Christ to it.

I decree and declare new and great opportunities are heading my way by the power in Jesus Christ.

I will wait for my better to come in the name of Jesus Christ.

No good thing will God withhold from me.

I decree the new year will bring blessings in the name of Jesus Christ.

I will start this new day on top in Jesus Christ name.

I will not let depression enter my life in the name of Jesus Christ.

I declare restoration in my life in the name of Jesus Christ.

It was good for me to be afflicted so that I might learn His decrees. — Psalm 119:71 (NIV)

God has a more fantastic assignment for my life.

I decree that my story shall end victoriously in the name of Jesus Christ.

For I know the plans I have for you, declares the Lord, plans for welfare and not for evil, to give you a future and hope. Then you will call upon me and come and pray to me, and I will hear you. You will seek me and find me when you seek me with all your heart. — Jeremiah 29:11-13 (ESV)

God is not done with me yet!

I shall praise God for my breakthrough because He has already provided!

It's already done in Jesus Christ name. Amen.

Father, in the name of Jesus Christ, I bless and praise thee Oh God. I decree and declare that I will not feel rejection when…

_____

_____

_____

_____

_____

_____

_____

_____

_____

_____

_____

_____

CHAPTER SIX

Dealing with Covetous

Tell me something, if you could have the home of anyone, who would it be? If you could have anyone's musical talents, who would it be? If you could have anyone's physical appearance, who would you look like? If you could have anyone's bank accounts, who would you choose? If you could marry anyone, married or single, who would it be? If you could have someone's spiritual anointing, who would it be? If you answered any of those questions, congratulations, you are a coveter. Now ask yourself, who are you hurting while you are coveting? Yes, you guessed right, yourself and God.

The last commandment of the Ten Commandment states, "Thou shalt not covet thy neighbor's house, thou shalt not covet thy neighbor's wife, nor his manservant, nor his maidservant, nor his ox, nor his ass, nor anything that is thy neighbor's (Exodus 20:17)." Coveting is a private sin. Remember, sin starts in the heart, where you internalize the desire and then act on it. It's like cause and effect. You want something that belongs to someone else in your heart, and then you go and take it. In other words, when you don't like what the Father has in store for you, you start coveting the plans that He has for someone else. God sees your heart.

I reject the spirit of covetousness in the name of Jesus Christ.

Thou shalt not covet thy neighbor's house, thou shalt not covet thy neighbor's wife, nor his manservant, nor his maidservant, nor his ox, nor his ass, nor anything that is thy neighbor's. — Exodus 20:17

For the commandments, "You shall not commit adultery, You shall not murder, You shall not steal, You shall not covet," and any other commandment, are summed up in this word: "You shall love your neighbor as yourself." — Romans 13:9 (NKJV)

In the name of Jesus Christ, Father, please forgive me for coveting.

In the name of Jesus Christ, Father, please forgive me for evil thoughts and intentions in my heart.

Put to death, therefore, what is earthly in you: sexual immorality, impurity, passion, evil desire, and covetousness, which is idolatry. — Colossians 3:5 (NIV)

I will guard my heart in the name of Jesus Christ.

I denounce demonic voices in my mind in the name of Jesus Christ.

I will ignore my negative thoughts.

I will speak what thus says the Lord.

I will not hold a conversation with evil spirits in the name of Jesus Christ.

I denounce the desire in my heart to sin in the name of Jesus Christ.

Lord, let me see the sin of covetousness in my life in the name of Jesus Christ.

Father, in the name of Jesus Christ, teach me how to stay on my guard for covetousness.

Father, clean my mind and purify my heart in the name of Jesus Christ.

Father, in the name of Jesus Christ, let me have a steadfast and sound mind.

And he said to them, "Take care, and be on your guard against all covetousness, for one's life does not consist in the abundance of his possessions." — Luke 12:15 (ESV)

For you may be sure of this, that everyone who is sexually immoral or impure, or who is covetous (that is, an idolater), has no inheritance in the Kingdom of Christ and God. — Ephesians 5:5 (ESV)

You desire and do not have, so you murder. You covet and cannot obtain, so you fight and quarrel. You do not have, because you do not ask. — James 4:2 (ESV)

Let covetousness not be named upon me in the name of Jesus Christ.

I denounce covetousness, making me lose my place in the Kingdom of God in the name of Jesus Christ.

I bind up the poison of coveting in the name of Jesus Christ.

I cancel the wrong attitude towards material things in Jesus Christ name.

I bind up the desire and greed for material gains in Jesus Christ name.

But sexual immorality and all impurity or covetousness must not even be named among you, as is proper among saints. — Ephesians 5:3 (ESV)

I cancel putting worldly things in front of God.

I decree that I will have the wisdom to store up treasure in heaven in the name of Jesus Christ.

I know that God has already given me everything I need.

I know that God will satisfy me.

Therefore, consider the members of your earthly body as dead to immorality, impurity, passion, evil desire, and greed, which amounts to idolatry. — Colossians 3:5 (NASB)

Make sure that your character is free from the love of money, being content with what you have; for He Himself has said, "I will never desert you, nor will I ever forsake you," — Hebrews 13:5 (NASB)

What shall we say then? Is the Law sin? May it never be! On the contrary, I would not have come to know sin except through the Law; for I would not have known about coveting if the Law had not said, "You shall not covet." — Romans 7:7 (NKJV)

It's OK To Be Single

But actually, I wrote to you not to associate with any so-called brother if he is an immoral person, or covetous, or an idolater, or a reviler, or a drunkard, or a swindler—not even to eat with such a one. — 1 Corinthians 5:11 (NASB)

I will keep my eyes on the calling placed upon me in the name of Jesus Christ.

I command my life to come into order in the name of Jesus Christ.

I bind the temptation of coveting in the name of Jesus Christ.

I claim I will have contentment in Jesus Christ.

I claim joy in the name of Jesus Christ.

I will not quit the faith in the name of Jesus Christ.

I will have self-control in the name of Jesus Christ.

I have made up my mind to follow Jesus Christ.

I cancel being a people pleaser in the name of Jesus Christ.

I need your help to get through the deliverance of coveting.

In the name of Jesus Christ, Father, I thank You for the deliverance from unhealthy cravings.

I don't have to have the things I want, Father; I am enough.

I rebuke my evil desires in the name of Jesus Christ.

Father, I need You. I need Your help to shake it off.

Oh, God, take away this craving in my heart.

I claim contentment in all the seasons of my life in the name of Jesus Christ.

Father, in the name of Jesus Christ, I know that You will never leave me.

Above all else, guard your heart, for everything you do flows from it. Keep your mouth free of perversity;

keep corrupt talk far from your lips. Let your eyes look straight ahead; fix your gaze directly before you. Give careful thought to the paths for your feet and be steadfast in all your ways. Do not turn to the right or the left; keep your foot from evil. — Proverbs 4:23-27 (NIV)

I will check my heart's desires in the name of Jesus Christ.

But the things that come out of a person's mouth come from the heart, and these defile them. — Matthew 15:18 (NIV)

I rebuke the spirit of greed in the name of Jesus Christ.

I reclaim joy in my life in the name of Jesus Christ.

I will not let desires conquer me.

I will admit that I need the help of the Father to shake this desire.

In the name of Jesus Christ, Father, please help me stay on track with Your desires for my life.

I bind up a corrupt mind in the name of Jesus Christ.

I rebuke vain imaginations in the name of Jesus Christ.

I rebuke the voice of the evil ones in my ears in the name of Jesus Christ.

I rebuke the visual aids the evil ones place in front of my eyes in the name of Jesus Christ.

Father, in the name of Jesus Christ, please show me how to love myself.

"For I know the plans I have for you," declares the LORD, "Plans to prosper you and not to harm you, plans to give you hope and a future." — Jeremiah 29:11 (NIV)

I will not lust after someone else's blessing in the name of Jesus Christ.

I will stay on the path God has planned for me in the name of Jesus Christ.

I will stay connected to the power of God in the name of Jesus Christ.

I denounce the carnal mind in the name of Jesus Christ.

Let your conversation be without covetousness; and be content with such things as ye have: for he hath said, I will never leave thee, nor forsake thee. So that we may boldly say, The Lord is my helper, and I will not fear what man shall do unto me. — Hebrew 13:5-6

I thank You for deliverance from cravings in the name of Jesus Christ.

I will walk in love in the name of Jesus Christ.

Not that I speak in respect of want: for I have learned, in whatsoever state I am, therewith to be content. I know both how to be abased, and I know how to abound: everywhere and in all things I am instructed both to be full and to be hungry, both to abound and to suffer need. — Philippians 4:11-12

I will stay in my lane in this life.

I am delivered from covetousness in Jesus Christ. Amen.

Father, in the name of Jesus Christ, I bless and praise thee Oh God. I decree and declare that I will not covet over…

_____

_____

_____

_____

_____

_____

_____

_____

_____

_____

_____

_____

_____

_____

It's OK To Be Single

CHAPTER SEVEN

Dealing with Word Curses

In the beginning was the Word (John 1:1). You see, everything starts with A WORD. God, who is our source, used words to create, and you can do the same thing. Word curses are hurtful words spoken over a person that opens up the gates for the devil to have legal rights. When you hear hurtful words spoken over you, you must immediately denounce them before they alter your existence. These words could potentially damage your self-esteem and even hinder the plans God has for you (Jeremiah 29:11).

It will be your decision on what words you let manifest in your reality. Words carry power, whether good or evil. So when you hear them, start binding them up on the spot.

I reject word curses over my life in the name of Jesus Christ.

I remove the effects of the word curses in the name of Jesus Christ.

I cancel all word curses and attacks from the enemy in Jesus Christ name.

I remove slander that was spoken over my life in the name of Jesus Christ.

Wherefore God also hath highly exalted him, and given him a name which is above every name: That at the name of Jesus every knee should bow, of things in heaven, and things in earth, and things under the earth; — Philippians 2:9-10

Every word curse in my life has to bow down that highly exalted name of Jesus Christ.

Please, Lord, forgive me for allowing word curses to rule over my life.

I repent of all my sins in the name of Jesus Christ.

Thank You for removing word curses over my life.

Thank you, Father, for walking with me.

Father, forgive me for not following Your commandments.

I revoke evil decrees against me in the name of Jesus Christ.

I bind up evil decrees over my life in the name of Jesus Christ.
Father, remove the people in my life that speak evil over me in the name of Jesus Christ.

I cast down evil proclamations over my life.

No weapon formed against me shall prosper.

I pull down false utterances in the mighty name of Jesus Christ.

I break demonic word curses over me in the name of Jesus Christ.

I break word curses over generations of my bloodline in the name of Jesus Christ.

Father, bless me with wisdom to deal with people who cursed me in the name of Jesus Christ.

I break the oppression over my life due to word curses in the name of Jesus Christ.

I rebuke good and bad intentions of word curses over my life in the name of Jesus Christ.

Everything the thief is trying to destroy, I rebuke in the name of Jesus Christ.

I denounce the atmosphere the word curse manifested itself in; in the name of Jesus Christ

I break family curses.

I break witchcraft curses.

I denounce legal rights to demonic spirits in the name of Jesus Christ.

I cancel all spells, hexes, vexes, and witchcraft in the mighty name of Jesus Christ.

I denounce all word curses spoken over me by authority figures in the name of Jesus Christ.

Expose witchcraft in the name of Jesus Christ.

I receive the words that God has spoken over me.

I come against word curses over my life in the name of Jesus Christ.

I bind up words that curse me in the name of Jesus Christ.

I will decree positive words in my life, and it shall be done unto me in the name of Jesus Christ.

I rebuke the word curse in my bloodline in the name of Jesus Christ.

He who guards his mouth preserves his life, but he who opens wide his lips shall have destruction. — Proverb 13:3 (NKJV)

I will be careful what comes out of my mouth by the power of the blood of Jesus Christ.

I will learn to control my mouth to protect my life.

I will not speak destructive words in the name of Jesus Christ.

And that ye study to be quiet, and to do your own business, and to work with your own hands, as we commanded you; — 1 Thessalonians 4:11

Death and life are in the power of the tongue, And those who love it will eat its fruit. — Proverbs 18.21 (NASB)

What you say can preserve life or destroy it, so you must accept the consequences of your words. — Proverbs 18:21 (GNT)

I rebuke and bind up self-curses in the name of Jesus Christ.

I break every word curse that my parents spoke over me in the name of Jesus Christ.

I will forgive in the name of Jesus Christ.

I will pay attention to the words that exit my mouth in the name of Jesus Christ.

I will speak life in the name of Jesus Christ.

I will speak peace in the name of Jesus Christ.

I will speak love in the name of Jesus Christ.

I cancel and cast out all witchcraft word curses towards me and send it to the abyss in the name of Jesus Christ.

I do not agree with any word curses in the name of Jesus Christ.

I bind up the family's familiar spirits in the name of Jesus Christ.

I will not attach myself to anything that will bring on curses in my life in the name of Jesus Christ.

Ye shall make you no idols nor graven image, neither rear you up a standing image, neither shall ye set up any image of stone in your land, to bow down unto it: for I am the Lord your God. — Leviticus 26:1

I will not receive any items that will curse my life in the name of Jesus Christ.

I will throw away any items that have any images that are not of God.

I will not bring items that will grieve the Holy Spirit in the name of Jesus Christ.

In the name of Jesus Christ, Father, please show me any items around me that are placing curses on me.

I break strongholds in the name of Jesus Christ.

Every spirit of lack must go in the name of Jesus Christ.

I will not be hard on myself in the name of Jesus Christ.

Father God, close the mouth of the devour.

Father, be my vindicator.

I bind the tongues of the gossipers in Jesus Christ name.

I bind poor word choices in the name of Jesus Christ.

I bind the hypothetical words spoken over me.

I restrict negative thoughts that arises in people's minds about me.

I release the anointing on my life in the name of Jesus Christ.

I decree that when I feel someone speaking evil over my life, I will rebuke it in the name of Jesus Christ.

Holy Spirit, convict and expose them to the world in the name of Jesus Christ.

I receive positive words throughout my life.

I break off the demonic mission that came to steal, kill, and destroy in the name of Jesus Christ.

I close every door to generational word curses over my family in the name of Jesus Christ.

I rebuke words against my future spouse and children in the name of Jesus Christ.

I denounce the evil words I spoke over myself in the name of Jesus Christ.

Break free in the name of Jesus Christ.

I cancel negativity from word curses in the mind in the name of Jesus Christ.

I cancel all word curses from my father and mother's father, grandfather, great grandfather up to the tenth generation in the name of Jesus Christ.

I cancel all word curses from my father and mother's mother, grandmother, great grandmother up to the tenth generation in the name of Jesus Christ.

I release faith in my life in the name of Jesus Christ.

In the name of Jesus Christ, Father, please protect me from all word curses in my past, present, and future.

I block any word curses that are spoken in secret in the name of Jesus Christ.

Forgive me, Father, for the word curse I placed on my own life and others.

To appoint unto them that mourn in Zion, to give unto them beauty for ashes, the oil of joy for mourning, the garment of praise for the spirit of heaviness; that they might be called trees of righteousness, the planting of the LORD, that he might be glorified. — Isaiah. 61:3

I decree that there is a blessing on the other side in the name of Jesus Christ.

I will close the door of the negative words I have spoken over myself in the name of Jesus Christ.

All word curses over my life is canceled in the mighty name of Jesus Christ.

I rebuke word curses that are stopping my dreams in the name of Jesus Christ.

Father, show me where the curses are coming from, so I can rebuke them in the name of Jesus Christ.

The Word of God is stronger than any evil word over my life.

There is power in my mouth through the authority of the Father.

I cast all the word curses into the abyss in the name of Jesus Christ.

The word curses can no longer work on me in the name of Jesus Christ.

I will walk in a curse free life in the name of Jesus Christ.

I command every curse to bow down to the blood of Jesus Christ.

Be broken now.

Thank you, Father, for undoing the curses.

I am set free. Amen.

Father, in the name of Jesus Christ, I bless and praise thee Oh God. I decree and declare that I will not let word curses...

_____

_____

_____

_____

_____

_____

_____

_____

_____

_____

CHAPTER EIGHT

Dealing with Thoughts

Unwanted thoughts can occur suddenly in your mind. These thoughts can be a powerful tool leading you back to your past and even getting stuck there. It also can produce the fear of being alone and cause you to do something you may regret. God equipped us with the spirit of power, love, and a sound mind to combat those thoughts. Reciting God's Words will help redirect your mind.

I renounce distraction from the past in the name of Jesus Christ.

No situation can keep me from the love of Christ Jesus.

No, I will not fall back into a toxic relationship.

No, I will not stop my progression for old memories in the name of Jesus Christ.

Create in me a pure heart, O God, and renew a steadfast spirit within me. Do not cast me from your presence or take your Holy Spirit from me. Restore to me the joy of your salvation and grant me a willing spirit, to sustain me. — Psalm 51:10-12 (NIV)

And the Spirit of the Lord shall rest upon him, the spirit of wisdom and understanding, the spirit of counsel and might, the spirit of knowledge and of the fear of the Lord; — Isaiah 11:2

For God has not given us a spirit of fear, but of power and of love and of a sound mind. — 2 Timothy 1:7

I call on the Spirit of Might and Power in the name of Jesus Christ.

And be not conformed to this world: but be ye transformed by the renewing of your mind, that ye may prove what is good, and acceptable, and perfect, will of God. — Romans 12:2

Father, in the name of Jesus Christ, I thank You for keeping me focus on my new season.

Take every one of your thoughts (beliefs, imaginations, dreams, and ideas) captive to the obedience of Christ. — 2 Corinthians 10:5

Finally, brethren, whatsoever things are true, whatsoever things are honest, whatsoever things are just, whatsoever things are pure, whatsoever things are lovely, whatsoever things are of good report; if there be any virtue, and if there be any praise, think on these things. — Philippians 4:8

Be careful for nothing; but in everything by prayer and supplication with thanksgiving let your requests be made known unto God. — Philippians 4:6

I will renew my mind daily in the name of Jesus Christ.

Father, the Creator of my mind, I ask You to guard and direct my mind in the name of Jesus Christ.

I bind up self-defeating thoughts in the name of Jesus Christ.

Take my yoke upon you and learn from me, for I am gentle and humble in heart, and you will find rest for your souls. — Matthew 11:29

You were taught, with regard to your former way of life, to put off your old self, which is being corrupted by its deceitful desires; to be made new in the attitude of your minds; and to put on the new self, created to be like God in true righteousness and holiness. — Ephesians 4:22-24 (NIV)

I bind up distractions in the name of Jesus Christ.

I decree that I will renew my mind with positive thoughts towards my future.

Repent, then, and turn to God, so that your sins may be wiped out, that times of refreshing may come from the Lord. — Acts 3:19 (NIV)

Therefore if any man be in Christ, he is a new creature. The old things are passed away. Behold, all things are become new. — 2 Corinthians 5:17

I decree and declare that the love from the Father will shine through me wherever I go in the name of Jesus Christ.

I claim peace of mind in the name of Jesus Christ.

I will activate my talents in the name of Jesus Christ.

Rejoice in the Lord always; again I will say, rejoice! — Philippians 4:4

But let all who take refuge in You be glad, Let them ever sing for joy; And may You shelter them, That those who love Your name may exult in You. — Psalm 5:11 (NIV)

Be glad in the Lord and rejoice you righteous ones; And shout for joy, all you who are upright in heart. — Psalm 32:11 (NKJV)

Thank you, Father, for teaching me how to renew my mind. Amen.

Father, in the name of Jesus Christ, I bless and praise thee Oh God. I decree and declare that I will say "No" to...

_____

_____

_____

_____

_____

_____

_____

_____

_____

_____

_____

_____

CHAPTER NINE

Fasting and Praying

After you have done it all, and nothing is working, it's time to fast and pray. Mark 9:26 states, "And he said unto them, "This kind can come forth by nothing, but by prayer and fasting." Fasting has many benefits. It adds fuel to your prayers, removes strongholds, strengthens you, provides power, guarantees an answer, changes you, drives out evil, breaks habits and mental bondages, speeds up healing, quiets the heart, brings you closer to the Father through Jesus Christ and much more.

Fasting is something between you and God. Isaiah 58:6 states, "Is not this the fast that I have chosen? To loose the bands of wickedness, to undo the heavy burdens, and to let the oppressed go free, and that ye break every yoke?" Let Him lead you into the fast. Daniel only consumed vegetables and water for ten days and abstained from delicacies for twenty-one days (Daniel 1:12 & Daniel 10: 2-3). Whatever instructions the Father gives you that is what you should do.

If you decide to do a fast that eliminates food, please consult your physician.

I claim the supernatural power of fasting and praying in the name of Jesus Christ.

I will seek the Lord on what fast to be on in the name of Jesus Christ.

I renounce the control of my flesh over my spirit in the name of Jesus Christ.

I break any strongholds on my neck in the name of Jesus Christ.

I decree breakthroughs in the name of Jesus Christ.

I decree and declare that mountains move in the name of Jesus Christ.

So we fasted and besought our God for this: and he was intreated of us. — Ezra 8:23

I will set myself before God.

I will humble myself in the presence of God.

Thank you, Father, for guiding me in Jesus Christ name.

And I set my face unto the Lord God, to seek by prayer and supplications, with fasting, and sackcloth, and ashes: And I prayed unto the Lord my God, and made my confession, and said, O Lord, the great and dreadful God, keeping the covenant and mercy to them that love him, and to them that keep his commandments; We have sinned, and have committed iniquity, and have done wickedly, and have rebelled, even by departing from thy precepts and from thy judgments: — Daniel 9:3-5

I decree that I will dedicate time for prayer in the name of Jesus Christ.

Moreover, when you fast, do not be like the hypocrites, with a sad countenance. For they disfigure their faces that they may appear to men to be fasting. Assuredly, I say to you, they have their reward. But you, when you fast, anoint your head and wash your face, so that you do not appear to men to be fasting, but to your Father who is in the secret place; and your Father who sees in secret will reward you openly. — Matthew 6:16-18

I will put on a happy face during my fasting period in the name of Jesus Christ.

I decree and declare that healing will be the result of this fast in the name of Jesus Christ.

Thank you, Father, for freeing up time for me to pray.

I rebuke frustration in the name of Jesus Christ.

I come against the spirit of oppression in the name of Jesus Christ.

As they ministered to the Lord and fasted, the Holy Ghost said, Separate me Barnabas and Saul for the work whereunto I have called them. And when they had fasted and prayed and laid their hands on them, they sent them away. So they, being sent forth by the Holy Ghost, departed unto Seleucia; and from thence they sailed to Cyprus. — Acts 13:2-4

I will seek direction from the Lord on this fast in the name of Jesus Christ.

Sanctify ye a fast, call a solemn assembly, gather the elders and all the inhabitants of the land into the house of the Lord your God, and cry unto the Lord. — Joel 1:14

Therefore also now, saith the Lord, turn ye even to me with all your heart, and with fasting, and with weeping, and with mourning: And rend your heart, and not your garments, and turn unto the Lord your God: for he is gracious and merciful, slow to anger, and of great kindness, and repenteth him of the evil. — Joel 2:12-13

Then there came some that told Jehoshaphat, saying, There cometh a great multitude against thee from beyond the sea on this side Syria; and, behold, they be in Hazazontamar, which is Engedi. And Jehoshaphat feared, and set himself to seek the Lord, and proclaimed a fast throughout all Judah. — 2 Chronicles 20:2-3

At the beginning of thy supplications the commandment came forth, and I am come to shew thee; for thou art greatly beloved: therefore understand the matter, and consider the vision. Seventy weeks are determined upon thy people and upon thy holy city, to finish the transgression, and to make an end of sins, and to make reconciliation for iniquity, and to bring in everlasting righteousness, and to seal up the vision and prophecy, and to anoint the most Holy. — Daniel 9:23-24

Thank you, Father, in the name of Jesus Christ for answering my prayers. Amen.

Father, in the name of Jesus Christ, I bless and praise thee Oh God. I decree and declare that I will fast and pray for…

CHAPTER TEN

Getting to Know You

Now it's time to get to know who you are while you are by yourself. Pull out a notepad and answer these questions: What is my value? Am I happy? What are my strength and weaknesses? What are my short and long-term goals? Am I caring for myself? What do I like to do? What am I worried about? What am I afraid of? When was the last time I took myself out? Am I walking in my calling? Now you are breaking up the pattern of not considering yourself.

Not knowing who you are, your worth, or your value is not healthy. If you don't know your worth, it will be hard for others to gauge it, and you don't want people to dictate how you feel about yourselves. The enemy doesn't want you to know who you are and the power you hold, so you have to stay close to God to be successful. God will take care of you in the process.

I cancel all circumstances that turned me into someone I am not.

I am comfortable in my skin.

I am proud of myself.

I am proud of the work I do.

Fret not thyself because of evildoers, neither be thou envious against the workers of iniquity. — Psalms 37:1

I work in excellence in the name of Jesus Christ.

Be strong and of good courage, fear not, nor be afraid of them: for the LORD thy God, he [it is] that doth go with thee; he will not fail thee, nor forsake thee. — Deuteronomy 31:6

This next decade will be great in the name of Jesus Christ.

I am worthy of life.

I am happy.

I love myself.

Thou shalt not avenge, nor bear any grudge against the children of thy people, but thou shalt love thy neighbor as thyself: I am the LORD. — Leviticus 19:18

A new commandment I give unto you, That ye love one another; as I have loved you, that ye also love one another. — John 13:34

As the Father hath loved me, so have I loved you: continue ye in my love. — John 15:9

I have peace in my life by the power of Jesus Christ.

Peace I leave with you, my peace I give unto you: not as the world giveth, give I unto you. Let not your heart be troubled, neither let it be afraid. — John 14:27

I will invest in myself.

I will invest in capitalizing on my gifts in the name of Jesus Christ.

For no man ever yet hated his own flesh; but nourisheth and cherisheth it, even as the Lord the church: — Ephesians 5:29

For we are his workmanship, created in Christ Jesus unto good works, which God hath before ordained that we should walk in them. — Ephesians 2:10

Likewise, the spirit also helpeth our infirmities: for we know not what we should pray for as we ought: but the spirit itself maketh intercession for us with groanings which cannot be uttered. — Romans 8:26

I will listen to the small still voice in the name of Jesus Christ.

I will get to know myself physically, mentally, and emotionally.

I will work on my inside in the name of Jesus Christ.

But the LORD said unto Samuel, Look not on his countenance, or on the height of his stature; because I have refused him: for [the LORD seeth] not as man seeth; for man looketh on the outward appearance, but the LORD looketh on the heart. — 1 Samuel 16:7

Father, in the name of Jesus Christ, please show me my worth.

Father, reveal to me my strengths and weaknesses.

I will experience a breakthrough in my life in the name of Jesus Christ.

I cancel flipping out on people in the name of Jesus Christ.

I cast down worry in the name of Jesus Christ.

Therefore I say unto you, Take no thought for your life, what ye shall eat, or what ye shall drink; nor yet for your body, what ye shall put on. Is not the life more than meat, and the body than raiment? — Matthew 6:25

But seek ye first the Kingdom of God, and his righteousness, and all these things shall be added unto you. — Matthew 6:33

Casting all your care upon him; for he careth for you. — 1 Peter 5:7

I can do all things through Christ, which strengtheneth me. — Philippians 4:13

Heaviness in the heart of man maketh it stoop: but a good word maketh it glad.—Proverbs 12:25

Humble yourselves therefore under the mighty hand of God, that he may exalt you in due time: — 1 Peter 5:6 (NIV)

Come unto me, all [ye] that labour and are heavy laden, and I will give you rest. — Matthew 11:28

Which of you by taking thought can add one cubit unto his stature? — Matthew 6:27

Cast thy burden upon the LORD, and he shall sustain thee: he shall never suffer the righteous to be moved. — Psalms 55:22

I will not be afraid of what God shows me about myself in the name of Jesus Christ.

There is no fear in love; but perfect love casteth out fear: because fear hath torment. He that feareth is not made perfect in love. — 1 John 4:18

Be careful for nothing; but in every thing by prayer and supplication with thanksgiving, let your requests be made known unto God. Philippians 4:6

But my God shall supply all your needs according to his riches in glory by Christ Jesus. — Philippians 4:19

I will consult God on my journey in understanding myself in the name of Jesus Christ.

I will walk with confidence in Jesus Christ name.

I will reach my goals in the name of Jesus Christ.

I will focus on my hope in the name of Jesus Christ.

I will live on purpose.

I will give myself special attention to understand my strengths and weaknesses, talents, passions, and purpose.

I will fulfill my true genius in me.

I will know my actual value and worth in life.

I will figure out what motivates me to get up in the morning.

I will figure out the things that come to me naturally that I can do very well.

I will conquer my fears through the power of Jesus Christ.

I will receive the message that God wants me to get across to people.

Circumstances nor people will run my life. The Father will run my life.

I will become what God has ordained me to be.

I will trust my vision.

I will write down what I want, think about it, reject images I can't do, and form positive images in my mind.

If needed, I will seek advice from an expert.

I will work on my countenance.

I will dress modestly for the glory of God.

I will set the tone for my life.

I will start that business in the name of Jesus Christ.

I will write that book in the name of Jesus Christ.

I will concentrate on my health in the name of Jesus Christ.

I will stay aware of what I am cooking and eating.

I will exercise more often.

My body will model a Godly body in the name of Jesus Christ.

I will participate in God approved extracurricular activities that I am interested in by the power of Jesus Christ.

I am worthy of having good things.

I do not have to settle for less.

I thank You, God, for the new relationship shortly.

Father, I will wait on your perfect timing.

Thank You, Father, for preparing me for the next relationship.

I thank God for finding myself in Him. Amen.

Father in the name of Jesus Christ, I bless and praise thee Oh God. I decree and declare that I will get to know myself...

_____
_____
_____
_____
_____
_____
_____
_____
_____
_____
_____
_____
_____
_____
_____
_____
_____
_____

CHAPTER ELEVEN

Single's Opportunities

Today you are single; this is the perfect time to explore new journeys with your creativity, personal growth, spirituality, financial stability, relaxation, just to name a few. It's an opportunity to establish yourself and fill your life with meaningful and enjoyable things such as spending quality time with friends, advancing your career, owning a home, exploring the world, taking music lessons, or whatever you desire.

Now is the perfect time to gather all your spiritual growth in Christ.

Thank you, Father, for giving me the opportunity in my singleness to get myself together in the name of Jesus Christ.

I release the spirits of love, power, and a sound mind in the name of Jesus Christ.

I cast out all delays in the name of Jesus Christ.

I bind limited opportunities in the name of Jesus Christ.

As we have therefore opportunity, let us do good unto all men, especially unto them who are of the household of faith. — Galatians 6:10

I claim every opportunity I pursue expands to more excellent opportunities in the name of Jesus Christ.

I receive Godly opportunities to come my way in the name of Jesus Christ.

For, brethren, ye have been called unto liberty; only use not liberty for an occasion to the flesh, but by love serve one another. — Galatians 5:13

Making the most of your time because the days are evil. — Ephesians 5:16

I will spend my time wisely in Jesus Christ.

I will create new opportunities for myself and others in the name of Jesus Christ.

My life is full of unlimited possibilities in the name of Jesus Christ.

Be wise in the way you act toward outsiders, making the most of the opportunity. — Colossians 4:5

I will be confident in the name of Jesus Christ.

I decree and declare that I will preach the word; be instant in season, out of season; reprove, rebuke, exhort with all longsuffering and doctrine. — 2 Timothy 4:2

You, my brothers and sisters, were called to be free. But do not use your freedom to indulge the sinful nature; rather, serve one another humbly in love. — Galatians 5:13

I command all stubborn opportunities to open in the name of Jesus Christ.

I decree that God will walk with me.

The opportunities that come are for my good.

I rebuke my enemies that bring trouble around my opportunities.

I rebuke the tricks of the enemy.

I can achieve greatness in the name of Jesus Christ.

Great opportunities to meet influential people are coming my way in the name of Jesus Christ.

Seeing therefore it remaineth that some must enter therein, and they to whom it was first preached entered not in because of unbelief. — Hebrews 4:6

And I will keep on doing what I am doing in order to cut the ground from under those who want an opportunity to be considered equal with us in the things they boast about.— 2 Corinthians 11:12 (NIV)

But I rejoiced in the Lord greatly, that now at the last your care of me hath flourished again; wherein ye were also careful, but ye lacked opportunity. — Philippians 4:10

Walk-in wisdom toward them that are without, redeeming the time. — Colossians 4:5

And truly, if they had been mindful of that country from whence they came out, they might have had opportunity to have returned. — Hebrew 11:15

I rebuke hindering spirits towards my opportunities.

Thank you, Father, for restoring opportunities.

For sin, taking occasion by the commandment, deceived me, and by it slew me. — Romans 7:11

I decree that I will walk in the direction of Godly opportunity.

I seize all Godly opportunities that come into my life in the name of Jesus Christ.

Oh Lord, if I have found favor in your sight, do not pass by your servant. —Genesis 18:3

I plead the blood of Jesus Christ over all of God's opportunities to run smoothly. Amen.

Father in the name of Jesus Christ, I bless and praise thee Oh God. I decree and declare that I will be grateful in my singleness. I will…

_____

_____

_____

_____

_____

_____

_____

_____

_____

_____

CHAPTER TWELVE

The "I am" Code

Exodus 3:14 states, "And God said unto Moses, I AM THAT I AM: and he said; thus shalt thou say unto the children of Israel, I AM hath sent me unto you." In this Scripture, God wanted to reassure Moses and Israel that He would be what they needed Him to be at any point on their journey. This assurance of God being what you need is for you.

Jesus Christ also uses the "I am Code" in His life.

- And Jesus said to them, "I am the bread of life. He who comes to Me shall never hunger, and he who believes in Me shall never thirst." — John 6:35
- Then Jesus spoke to them again, saying, "I am the light of the world. He who follows Me shall not walk in darkness, but have the light of life." — John 8:12
- "I am the door. If anyone enters by Me, he will be saved, and will go in and out and find pasture." — John 10:9
- "I am the good shepherd. The good shepherd gives His life for the sheep." — John 10:11
- Jesus said to her, "I am the resurrection and the life. He who believes in Me, though he may die, he shall live. And whoever lives and believes in Me shall never die. Do you believe this?" — John 11:25, 26
- Jesus said to him, "I am the way, the truth, and the life. No one comes to the Father except through Me." — John 14:6
- "I am the vine, you are the branches. He who abides in Me, and I in him, bears much fruit; for without Me you can do nothing." — John 15:5

Every word that followed "I am" Jesus Christ fulfilled it. Now it is time for you to speak into the atmosphere what you want to fulfill in your life.

I am putting my trust in God.

I am a servant of God.

I am a friend of God.

I am putting the Father first.

I am wonderfully made.

I am comfortable in my skin.

I am anointed.

I am moving on with my life.

I am wise.

I am a praiser.

I am a faith carrier.

I am a worshipper.

I am understanding.

I am grateful.

I am at peace.

I am valuable.

I am lovable.

I am healthy.

I am wealthy.

I am Knowledgeable.

I am a queen/king.

I am comfortable in my skin.

I am God's child.

I am fearless.

I am creative.

I am attractive.

I am open-minded.

I am wonderful.

I am honest.

I am healed.

I am loved.

I am a wife/husband.

I am called to Kingdom work.

I am making my vision big.

I am a child of the highest God.

I am headed in the right direction.

I am doing big things for Jesus Christ.

I am happy.

I am fun.

I am excellent in my ministry.

I am successful.

I am an entrepreneur.

I am a big tither.

I am a cheerful giver.

I am where I want to be financially.

I am a great leader.

I am recognized positively.

I am on time.

I am worth it.

I am a great writer.

I am a great cook.

I am bringing a positive and helpful attitude. Amen.

Father in the name of Jesus Christ, I bless and praise thee Oh God. I decree and declare that I am...

_____

_____

I am

_____

_____

I am

_____

_____

I am

_____

_____

I am

_____

_____

I am

_____

_____

I am

_____

_____

I am

_____

_____

I am

_____

_____

I am

_____

_____

I am

_____

_____

I am

_____

_____

CHAPTER THIRTEEN

Wait

Lamentations 3:25-26 states, "The Lord is good to those who wait for Him, to the soul who seeks Him. It is good that one should hope and wait quietly for the salvation of the Lord."

It is best to wait for God to position you so your spouse can see you. While you are waiting on your kingdom spouse, God places hope in you. He doesn't give you hope to be stagnant, but for you to work your faith until it manifest. Hope will give you victory.

Now walk in your divine purpose and watch God bring forth His promises.

Father in the name of Jesus Christ, I bless and praise thee Oh God. I decree and declare that I will wait with…

_____

_____

_____

_____

_____

_____

_____

_____

_____

_____

_____

_____

_____

_____

_____

About the Author

M.A. Jackson is a woman of God that enjoys encouraging people. Her passion is teaching the Word of God with simplicity. God blessed her to start MJ Ministries, preaching the Word to those unable to attend Sunday Services. She served in different ministries such as Youth Ministry Assistant, Church Program Coordinator, Drama Team Member, and a Praise and Worship Team Leader.

Keep in touch with MJ Ministries via the web:

Facebook:https://www.facebook.com/mel.jack.3950
Instagram: @mj_ministries
Youtube: MJ Ministries
TikTok: @mjministries

Index

A

abandoning, 23
abandonment, 55, 61
abased, 77
abides, 128
abundance, 70
abyss, 13, 30, 43, 56, 86, 91
acceptable, 96
acceptance, 56
access, 13
achieve, 35, 123
acknowledge, 1, 8, 14, 60
admit, 75

adultery, 69
afflicted, 17, 59, 64
afraid, 15, 62, 108, 110, 111, 114
aftermath, 31
agree, 8, 86
alone, 12, 16, 18, 19, 20, 56, 94
anger, 34, 36, 105
angered, 47
anointed, 129
anointing, 24, 67, 88
antidote, 12
anxieties, 20, 30
anxious, 20
ashes, 90, 103
ask, 3, 8, 35, 49, 56, 58, 68, 71, 97
assertive, 8
assignment, 64
assurance, 127
atmosphere, 83, 129
attention, 2, 4, 7, 10, 86, 115
attitude, 10, 22, 47, 71, 97, 133
attractive, 131
authority figures, 84
avenge, 29, 45, 110

B

bank accounts, 67

Barnabas, 105

beauty, 90

beliefs, 96

believes, 128

benefits, 101

better, 3, 42, 43, 48, 49, 63

big tither, 132

bind, 2, 13, 14, 35, 37, 61, 71, 73, 76, 82, 84, 86, 87, 88, 97, 121

bitterness, 36

blaming, 21

bless, 11, 29, 39, 46, 51, 53, 56, 65, 78, 83, 92, 99, 106, 118, 125, 133, 136

blessed, 34, 59, 137

blessing, 8, 18, 76, 90

blessings, 24, 29, 32, 34, 64

bloodline, 83, 85

boast, 124

body, 4, 7, 25, 72, 113, 117

bondage, 21, 50, 53

bondages, 101

Book, 6

books, 51

bow, 1, 2, 81, 82, 87, 92

branches, 128
brand new, 25
brawling, 36
breakthrough, 25, 50, 59, 65, 112
brokenness, 38
brothers, 123
Brothers, 49
burden, 24, 114
burdens, 19, 102
burned, 21
business, 85, 116
button, 13

C

calling, 51, 53, 73, 108
cancel, 4, 6, 15, 71, 72, 74, 81, 84, 86, 89, 90, 109, 112
cancellation, 2
capitalizing, 111
care, 3, 4, 5, 6, 7, 8, 9, 11, 46, 70, 109, 113, 124
career, 120
carnal, 15, 77
cast out, 2, 59, 86, 121
Casting, 20, 113
character, 72

chariot, 44

cheerful giver, 132

chest, 7

child, 60, 130, 131

children, 29, 89, 110, 127

choose, 8, 31, 63, 67

city, 59, 106

claim, 2, 6, 7, 8, 9, 10, 15, 17, 18, 23, 24, 34, 35, 36, 39, 43, 46, 57, 58, 59, 60, 61, 73, 74, 98, 102, 121

combat, 94

comfortable, 109, 129, 130

command, 2, 6, 56, 58, 73, 92, 123

commandment, 5, 68, 69, 106, 110, 124

commandments, 69, 82, 103

committed, 29, 43, 103

companionship, 17

company, 23, 58

compassion, 60, 61

compassionate, 36

concentrate, 116

concerns, 2

condemn, 2, 19

condemnation, 30, 32

confession, 103

confidence, 22, 56, 58, 114

conformed, 96

congregation, 4
conquer, 75, 115
consequences, 85
contentment, 73, 74
conversation, 70, 77
convict, 89
cook, 133
cooking, 117
corners, 9
corrupt, 75, 76
counsel, 95
countenance, 112, 116
courage, 36, 110
courageous, 15, 18
covenant, 103
covet, 68, 69, 71, 72, 78
covetous, 70, 73
covetousness, 68, 69, 70, 71, 77, 78
cravings, 74, 77
create, 42, 80, 122
creative, 131
creativity, 120

D

damage, 81

darkness, 128

day, 6, 10, 22, 24, 36, 52, 64

death, 69

decision, 81

decisions, 33, 36

declaration, 2

declare, 11, 14, 19, 24, 25, 26, 32, 33, 39, 53, 60, 61, 63, 64, 65, 78, 92, 98, 99, 103, 104, 106, 118, 122, 125, 133, 136

declining, 55

decree, 2, 4, 5, 6, 7, 9, 10, 11, 13, 16, 17, 23, 24, 25, 26, 32, 33, 35, 39, 44, 46, 53, 56, 57, 59, 63, 64, 65, 72, 78, 84, 88, 90, 92, 97, 98, 99, 103, 104, 106, 118, 122, 123, 124, 125, 133, 136

deeds, 13

defeated, 18

delicacies, 102

deliverance, 74, 77

delivered, 14, 78

delivering, 39

demonic, 58, 69, 83, 84, 89

demonic voices, 69

denial, 55

denounce, 2, 8, 9, 17, 25, 44, 48, 61, 69, 70, 71, 77, 80, 83, 84, 89

deny, 63

depart, 6, 59

depleting, 8

depression, 12, 21, 64

desire, 4, 7, 14, 16, 23, 25, 37, 68, 69, 70, 71, 72, 75, 120

desires, 74, 75, 97

destroy, 38, 83, 85, 89

destroyed, 24

die, 128

disappointment, 59

disciples, 6

disconnected, 12

disease, 57

dismayed, 18

dismissal, 55

disowning, 55

distraction, 95

distress, 14

doctrine, 122

doors, 51

doubt, 22

dreadful, 103

dreams, 91, 96

drunkard, 73

dust, 16, 59

dwelling, 19

E

ears, 76
earth, 1, 32, 81
eating, 4, 117
Egypt, 44
eliminate, 25
embrace, 22
emotional exhaustion, 9
emotions, 28, 38, 60
encourage, 23
encouraging, 22, 137
enemies, 29, 32, 56, 123
enemy, 29, 35, 46, 81, 109, 123
enlarged, 14
entrepreneur, 132
envious, 109
equipped, 94
errors, 30
eschew, 55
esteem, 59, 62, 81
events, 25
evil, 14, 28, 29, 45, 59, 60, 64, 69, 70, 72, 74, 75, 76, 81, 82, 88, 89, 91, 101, 105, 122
evildoers, 109

excellence, 109

excellent, 30, 121, 132

exclusion, 55

excuses, 23

exercise, 7, 117

exercising, 4

expert, 116

exquisite, 8

extracurricular activities, 117

extraordinary, 8

eye contact, 16

F

fail, 110

failure, 55

faith, 24, 73, 90, 121, 129, 135

faithful, 37, 48

false utterances, 83

familiar spirits, 87

family curses, 83

fast, 21, 53, 101, 102, 104, 105, 106

Fasting, 101, 102

father, 89, 90

Father, 1, 5, 11, 13, 14, 15, 16, 18, 20, 23, 25, 26, 29, 30, 31, 36, 38, 39, 43, 45, 46, 50, 53, 56, 60, 62, 63,

65, 68, 69, 70, 74, 75, 76, 78, 82, 83, 87, 88, 90, 91, 92, 96, 97, 98, 99, 102, 103, 104, 106, 110, 112, 116, 117, 118, 121, 124, 125, 128, 129, 133, 136

faults, 21

favor, 16, 125

fear, 18, 32, 46, 77, 94, 95, 110, 114

Fear, 18, 20

fearless, 130

feelings, 4, 7, 28, 39

feet, 16, 59, 75

fight, 13, 71

financial stability, 120

flame, 21

flesh, 102, 111, 122

flood, 46

flourish, 51

flow, 4

focus, 15, 49, 50, 51, 62, 96, 115

forgetting, 28, 33, 60

forgive, 30, 31, 32, 33, 36, 37, 38, 39, 45, 53, 56, 69, 82, 86

forgiven, 38

forgiveness, 30, 31, 38

Forgiveness, 28

forgotten, 4, 59

forsake, 15, 16, 18, 60, 72, 77, 110

free, 21, 29, 44, 53, 72, 74, 89, 91, 92, 102, 123

friends, 12, 13, 14, 23, 44, 50, 120

fruit, 85, 128

frustration, 104

fun, 132

future, 25, 33, 43, 47, 51, 57, 63, 64, 76, 89, 90, 97

G

gains, 71

garment, 90

gates, 80

generations, 83

genius, 115

gifts, 9, 111

glorified, 90

glory, 1, 46, 49, 57, 114, 116

Glory, 33

goal, 35, 49

goals, 108, 115

God, 1, 5, 6, 8, 9, 11, 13, 14, 15, 17, 18, 19, 20, 21, 22, 24, 25, 26, 28, 29, 33, 34, 37, 39, 43, 48, 49, 50, 53, 56, 57, 58, 59, 61, 63, 64, 65, 68, 71, 72, 74, 76, 77, 78, 80, 81, 84, 87, 88, 91, 92, 94, 95, 96, 97, 98, 99, 102, 103, 105, 106, 109, 110, 111, 113, 114, 115,

116, 117, 118, 123, 125, 127, 129, 130, 131, 133, 135, 136, 137

Godly advice, 15

good, 4, 9, 19, 23, 24, 28, 29, 39, 55, 57, 59, 61, 63, 64, 81, 83, 96, 110, 111, 113, 117, 121, 123, 128, 135

good news, 55

gossip, 36

gossipers, 88

gracious, 17, 105

grandfather, 89

grandmother, 90

grateful, 125, 130

graven image, 87

great grandfather, 89

great grandmother, 90

great leader, 132

greens, 7

grievance, 39

grieve, 87

groanings, 111

grudge, 110

guard, 20, 69, 70, 74, 97

guiding, 31, 103

H

habit, 22, 38
happiness, 3, 50
happy, 104, 108, 110, 132
happy face, 104
hate, 29, 37, 58
healed, 51, 62, 131
healing, 101, 104
health, 4, 12, 116
healthy, 4, 7, 10, 109, 130
heart, 5, 14, 17, 21, 25, 31, 32, 39, 64, 68, 69, 70, 74, 75, 95, 97, 99, 102, 105, 111, 112, 113
hearts, 20
heaven, 1, 29, 72, 81
heavens, 32
heavenward, 49
heaviness, 90
heavy laden, 19, 113
help, 4, 13, 18, 33, 36, 38, 44, 50, 51, 74, 75, 94
helper, 19, 77
heritage, 19
hexes, 84
hobby, 61
holiness, 97
Holy Ghost, 18, 31, 33, 105
Holy Spirit, 87, 89, 95
home, 67, 120

honest, 96, 131

honor, 7, 8

hope, 51, 64, 76, 115, 135

house, 59, 68, 105

household, 121

humble, 97, 103

hunger, 128

hungry, 77

hurt, 31, 34, 36, 38, 46, 52, 53

hurtful words, 80

hurting, 31, 68

hypocrites, 104

hypothetical words, 88

I

idolater, 71, 73

idolatry, 69, 72

imaginations, 96

impulsive, 34

impure, 70

impurity, 69, 71, 72

indulge, 123

influential people, 123

inheritance, 71

iniquities, 32

iniquity, 103, 106, 109

instructions, 102

intentional process, 28

intentions, 69, 83

invest, 10, 111

investment, 4

isolated, 13

isolation, 17

Israelites, 44

J

Jehoshaphat, 106

Jesus, 1, 2, 4, 5, 6, 7, 8, 9, 10, 11, 13, 14, 15, 16, 17, 18, 19, 20, 21, 22, 23, 24, 25, 26, 30, 31, 32, 33, 34, 35, 36, 37, 38, 39, 43, 44, 45, 46, 47, 48, 49, 50, 51, 53, 56, 57, 58, 59, 60, 61, 62, 63, 64, 65, 68, 69, 70, 71, 72, 73, 74, 75, 76, 77, 78, 81, 82, 83, 84, 85, 86, 87, 88, 89, 90, 91, 92, 95, 96, 97, 98, 99, 102, 103, 104, 105, 106, 109, 110, 111, 112, 114, 115, 116, 117, 118, 121, 122, 123, 125, 127, 128, 129, 131, 133, 136

journey, 114, 127

joy, 21, 33, 35, 38, 49, 73, 75, 90, 95, 98, 99

joyful, 10

judgment, 19

just, 7, 10, 37, 44, 52, 59, 96, 120

K

kind, 36, 101
kindness, 105
Kingdom of Christ, 71
Kingdom of darkness, 39
kingdom spouse, 135
knee, 1, 2, 81
knowledge, 22, 95
Knowledgeable, 130

L

labor, 19
laugh, 7
Law, 5, 6, 72
learn, 7, 53, 64, 85, 97
legal rights, 80, 84
liberty, 21, 122
life, 2, 3, 13, 15, 16, 21, 22, 23, 24, 25, 29, 33, 35, 36, 38, 43, 50, 58, 62, 63, 64, 70, 73, 74, 75, 77, 81, 82, 83, 84, 85, 86, 87, 88, 89, 90, 91, 97, 110, 112, 113, 115, 116, 120, 122, 125, 127, 128, 129
like-minded, 17, 62
limitation, 33

limits, 28
lips, 75, 85
listen, 8, 111
loneliness, 13, 14, 15, 17, 18, 19, 20, 25
Loneliness, 12, 13, 25
lonely, 17, 25, 52
loneness, 26
longsuffering, 122
Lord, 5, 7, 14, 18, 19, 21, 23, 25, 29, 39, 44, 45, 46, 47, 52, 64, 69, 70, 77, 82, 87, 95, 98, 99, 102, 103, 105, 106, 111, 124, 125, 135
LORD, 1, 13, 15, 16, 21, 60, 76, 90, 110, 112, 114
lovable, 130
love, 4, 5, 6, 8, 29, 32, 34, 35, 39, 49, 50, 52, 57, 69, 72, 76, 77, 85, 86, 94, 95, 98, 103, 110, 114, 121, 122, 123
lovely, 96
lust, 76

M

M.A. Jackson, 137
maidservant, 68
malice, 36
manservant, 68
married, 67

marry, 67

measures, 7

meditate, 6

memories, 47, 95

men, 29, 58, 104, 121

mercy, 14, 30, 103

message, 115

mighty, 4, 6, 9, 15, 38, 83, 84, 91, 113

mind, 5, 12, 14, 22, 25, 35, 44, 50, 52, 63, 69, 70, 73, 76, 77, 89, 94, 95, 96, 97, 98, 99, 116, 121

minds, 20, 44, 88, 97

ministered, 105

ministry, 132

mirror, 3

mistake, 32

mistakes, 29, 33

money, 42, 72

mother, 16, 60, 89, 90

motivates, 115

mountains, 103

mourn, 51, 90

mourning, 90, 105

mouth, 6, 74, 75, 85, 86, 88, 91

multitude, 106

murder, 69, 71

music lessons, 120

musical talents, 67

N

name, 1, 2, 4, 5, 6, 7, 8, 9, 10, 11, 13, 14, 15, 16, 17, 18, 19, 20, 21, 22, 23, 24, 25, 26, 30, 31, 32, 33, 34, 35, 36, 37, 38, 39, 43, 44, 45, 46, 47, 48, 49, 50, 51, 53, 56, 57, 58, 59, 60, 61, 62, 63, 64, 65, 68, 69, 70, 71, 72, 73, 74, 75, 76, 77, 78, 81, 82, 83, 84, 85, 86, 87, 88, 89, 90, 91, 92, 95, 96, 97, 98, 99, 102, 103, 104, 105, 106, 109, 110, 111, 112, 114, 115, 116, 117, 118, 120, 121, 122, 123, 125, 133, 136

neck, 24, 103

negative, 15, 28, 35, 61, 69, 88, 91

negativity, 42, 62, 89

neighbor, 5, 29, 68, 69, 110

new creation, 32, 39

new creature, 98

new self, 97

new technology, 13

night, 4, 6, 9

non-acceptance, 55

O

obedience, 96

offended, 32, 33, 56

offender, 28

offense, 28, 29, 37

old self, 97

open-minded, 131

opportunities, 63, 121, 122, 123, 124, 125

opportunity, 23, 63, 120, 121, 122, 124

oppose, 34

oppression, 83, 105

orphans, 20

overcome, 13, 56, 61, 63

overflow, 20, 52

overwhelming, 8, 9

ox, 68

P

pain, 29, 52, 60, 62

parents, 61, 86

passion, 69, 72, 137

pasture, 128

paths, 14, 75

peace, 15, 20, 34, 35, 39, 50, 51, 58, 60, 86, 98, 110, 111, 130

peaceably, 29

peaceful, 10, 34

peacefulness, 25
people pleaser, 74
perish, 46
persecute, 29
personal growth, 120
personal hygiene, 4
petty, 34
Pharaoh, 44
physician, 102
place, 1, 29, 45, 48, 71, 76, 104
plans, 64, 68, 76, 81
poison, 71
positive, 22, 24, 52, 62, 84, 89, 97, 116, 133
positive affirmations, 52
possesses, 15
possibilities, 51, 122
power, 2, 6, 25, 31, 46, 49, 56, 57, 58, 60, 63, 77, 81, 85, 91, 94, 95, 101, 102, 109, 110, 115, 117, 121
power source, 2
powerful, 3, 52, 94
praise, 4, 11, 21, 26, 39, 53, 65, 78, 90, 92, 96, 99, 106, 118, 125, 133, 136
pray, 29, 32, 33, 52, 53, 64, 101, 104, 106, 111
prayer, 2, 14, 20, 96, 101, 103, 104, 114
praying, 102
preach, 122

preached, 123
preaching, 137
presence, 8, 95, 103
prize, 49, 53
problems, 9, 21, 58
proclamations, 82
progression, 95
promise, 31, 46
promises, 136
prophecy, 106
prophesy, 34, 35
Prophets, 5
prosper, 19, 76, 82
prosperous, 6
protect, 85, 90
proud, 109
provide, 6
provision, 22
pure, 95, 96
purify, 37, 70
purpose, 39, 56, 57, 115, 136

Q

quality time, 120
questions, 67, 108

R

rage, 36
read, 22, 51
rebelled, 103
rebuff, 55
rebuke, 2, 21, 25, 34, 36, 37, 38, 43, 61, 74, 75, 76, 83, 85, 86, 88, 89, 91, 104, 122, 123, 124
reclaim, 2, 75
red flags, 3, 8
redeemed, 20
redirection, 63
refreshing, 18, 98
refuge, 98
Refusal, 55
regrets, 45, 49
reject, 13, 16, 30, 35, 43, 56, 68, 81, 116
rejected, 62
rejection, 16, 55, 56, 57, 58, 59, 60, 61, 62, 63, 65
rejoice, 98, 99
relationships, 35, 43, 44, 45
relax, 9
relaxed, 10
relief, 10
renew, 25, 52, 95, 97, 99

renounce, 2, 95, 102

renunciation, 55

Repay, 28

repentance, 46

repudiation, 55

requests, 20, 96, 114

resentment, 28, 39

respect, 10, 77

responsive, 23

rest, 19, 50, 56, 95, 97, 113

restoration, 34, 64

Restore, 95

restored, 34

resurrection, 128

revelation, 29

revenge, 45

reviler, 73

riches, 57, 114

righteous, 18, 99, 114

righteously, 5

righteousness, 14, 19, 90, 97, 106, 113

rivers, 20

rooted, 12

rules, 28

S

sackcloth, 103
sacrifice, 22
sad countenance, 104
sadness, 13, 61
saints, 71
salvation, 95, 135
Saul, 105
scars, 42
scorpions, 46
season, 20, 49, 96, 122
secret, 90, 104
security, 13
self-belief, 6
self-belittling, 6
Self-care, 3
self-control, 73
selfish act, 4
self-neglect, 4
self-respect, 10
serpents, 46
servant, 125, 129
servants, 19
sexual immorality, 69, 71
sexually immoral, 70
shelter, 98

shepherd, 128
sick, 17
sight, 28, 125
single, 67, 120
singleness, 121, 125
sinning, 22
sins, 22, 30, 32, 36, 37, 82, 98, 106
sisters, 49, 123
situation, 2, 36, 48, 95
skin, 35, 109, 129, 130
slander, 36, 81
sleep, 4, 9
social events, 4
social media, 45, 51
social setting, 23
society, 13
song, 21
sorrow, 33
sorrows, 59
soul, 4, 5, 22, 25, 35, 46, 135
souls, 97
sound mind, 94
special, 7, 45, 115
spells, 84
spirit, 3, 13, 14, 18, 20, 25, 30, 43, 56, 58, 61, 68, 75, 88, 90, 94, 95, 102, 105, 111

spirituality, 120

spouse, 46, 89, 135

spurning, 55

stagnant, 135

stature, 112, 114

steadfast, 32, 70, 75, 95

steal, 69, 89

story, 64

strength, 5, 15, 21, 63, 108

strengthen, 18, 22, 24

strengths, 112, 115

stress, 10

strong, 15, 18, 19, 43, 110

strongholds, 15, 36, 87, 101, 103

stuck, 48, 94

study, 85

success, 6

successful, 109, 132

suddenly, 94

suffer, 20, 77, 114

suffering, 42

supplication, 20, 96, 114

supplications, 103, 106

support, 18, 48

surpasses, 20, 58

sustain, 95, 114

swindler, 73

T

talents, 98, 115
teach, 31, 70
teaching, 30, 99, 137
tears, 33
temptation, 73
temptations, 49
Ten Commandment, 68
tenth generation, 89, 90
terrified, 15
thanksgiving, 20, 96, 114
thief, 83
thoughts, 4, 7, 14, 15, 22, 45, 52, 60, 69, 88, 94, 96, 97
thrive, 24
throne, 4, 48
time, 4, 12, 23, 28, 42, 52, 53, 101, 104, 108, 113, 120, 121, 122, 124, 129, 132
tongue, 1, 19, 85
tongues, 88
torment, 114
torments, 58
toxic relationship, 95

transformed, 96
transgression, 106
treat, 5, 7, 61
troubles, 31, 34
trust, 12, 21, 50, 116, 129
trusts, 21
truth, 22, 29, 128

U

unbelief, 123
understand, 17, 106, 115
understanding, 14, 20, 58, 95, 114, 130
undetected, 12
unforgiveness, 30, 34, 38
unforgiving, 38
unfruitful, 43
unique, 62
unrighteousness, 37
upright, 99
upset, 42

V

vain imaginations, 76
valuable, 55, 130

vegetables, 102
vengeance, 28, 39, 45
veto, 55
vexes, 84
victorious, 24
victoriously, 64
vindicator, 88
virtue, 96
vision, 106, 116, 131
visit, 9
visual aids, 76
voice, 76, 111

W

warfare, 15
warning signs, 3
water, 102
waters, 20
weaknesses, 108, 112, 115
wealthy, 130
weapon, 19, 82
weapons, 15
weeping, 105
welfare, 64
well-being, 3, 4

wickedness, 102
wife, 68, 131
willing spirit, 95
wisdom, 8, 22, 72, 83, 95, 124
wise, 122, 129
witchcraft, 84, 86
witchcraft curses, 84
withhold, 63
womb, 60
wonderful, 131
wonderfully made, 129
word curses, 61, 81, 82, 83, 84, 86, 89, 90, 91, 92
Word of God, 13, 137
workmanship, 111
world, 49, 89, 96, 111, 120, 128
worry, 21, 112
worshipper, 130
worth, 47, 109, 112, 115, 132
wrath, 29, 45
writer, 132

Y

year, 34, 50, 64
yoke, 19, 21, 24, 97, 102

www.ingramcontent.com/pod-product-compliance
Lightning Source LLC
Chambersburg PA
CBHW072012110526
44592CB00012B/1277